CAREERS IN THE UNITED STATES SECRET SERVICE

THE UNITED STATES SECRET SERVICE is the oldest federal law enforcement agency in the nation and is recognized as one of the most elite in the world. It is a self-contained organization, not part of the FBI or CIA. At the mention of the Secret Service, most people conjure up images of big men in dark suits and sunglasses, surrounding the leader of the free world wherever he goes. Indeed, the agency has a long history of protecting not only presidents, but vice presidents, their families, foreign dignitaries, and even presidential hopefuls. However, this is only part of the Secret Service story.

The agency was initially created as a division of the Treasury Department. In the wake of the Civil War, there was a large quantity of phony money in circulation. In fact, it is estimated that more than one-third of American currency was counterfeit at the time. President Abraham Lincoln established the Secret Service to combat the problem and to ensure the integrity of the nation's financial infrastructure. Ironically, Lincoln signed the legislation creating the agency on April 14, 1865 – the very day John Wilkes Booth assassinated him. Yet, it would be another 36 years before the Secret Service assumed the responsibility of protecting American presidents.

Since its inception, the agency has been investigating and guarding against financial crimes, such as counterfeiting, identity theft, computer fraud, money laundering, and all types of financial fraud. It also took on anyone "perpetrating mass frauds against the government," which included the likes of the Ku Klux Klan, among others. In 2003, the Secret Service was transferred to the Department of Homeland Security. Today, it fights crime on a global scale, investigating a growing list of technology-based crimes, such as cyber-attacks against the nation's financial and telecommunications infrastructure, and technological attacks that hack into government systems.

It is not easy to get into the Secret Service. Even someone with a college degree, law enforcement experience, and existing clearance standing will find the hiring process challenging. It takes about a year to go through the full, very specific application process that includes numerous tests, both mental and physical. It does not help to have connections either. It does not matter who you know, there is no shortcut to the front of the line. There are a number of requirements, such as US citizenship, age, clean drug tests, good vision, and excellent health and physical fitness. Perhaps the important requirement is the ability to obtain top-secret security clearance. Only those who have led impeccable lives are considered. The terms may be tough, but they work. While the NSA, CIA, and FBI have all been infiltrated by devious foreign agents, the Secret Service has a clean record.

Successful recruits proceed to training. There are training programs for Secret Service special agents, totaling 27 weeks. The agency provides one-of-a-kind training, designed to prepare agents for the high level of responsibility they will take on. Making it this far does not guarantee entry to the Secret Service. Failure to pass any test along the way is cause for immediate disqualification. New special agents who do successfully get through training are assigned to posts in one of the agency's domestic field offices. It takes several years of experience in a field office before an agent is qualified to transfer to protective duty.

Officers in the Uniformed Division also go through months of rigorous training. Unlike special agents, who can be assigned to offices anywhere in the US or overseas, officers in the Uniformed Division are typically assigned to protect government buildings and embassies in and around Washington, DC.

A career with the Secret Service is more than a job. Each day is challenging and demanding, yet exciting and rewarding all at the same time. It takes hard work and dedication to prepare for this career, but those who have made it insist the effort is well worth it. The rewards start with great pay, great benefits, opportunities for travel, and fascinating work. First and foremost, it is an honor and a privilege to ensure the safety of the nation.

WHAT YOU CAN DO NOW

THE FIRST STEP TO BECOMING A SECRET SERVICE AGENT is to plan ahead. Ideally, you would prepare for the application process while still in high school. You will need a bachelor's degree to be considered for a position as a special agent (this requirement does not apply to uniformed agents). Though not an official requirement, preference is given to those who have majored in criminal justice or pre-law. The competition for positions is intense. To gain an edge over other candidates, seriously consider one of these majors as you explore college options.

Consult with your guidance counselor to make sure your curriculum meets college admissions requirements. This generally means four years of math, English, and science. Psychology and sociology courses can also be very useful. Keep your grades up. A GPA of 3.0 or higher is expected during your college career. You should aim for the same goal in high school.

Outside of class, you should join clubs that feature teamwork and social service. Volunteering is an excellent way to show that you care about your community and that you have the passion for social service.

Physical fitness is an important aspect of a career in the Secret Service. In fact, all applicants must pass a physical fitness test. Do not put off getting into shape. If you are serious about pursuing this career, get a physical from your doctor and start getting in the habit of working out on a regular basis. Your fitness routine should involve cardiovascular exercises, running, and weight training. Getting involved in a sport is a great way to further improve your fitness while at the same time building teamwork skills.

How is your eyesight? Applicants must have uncorrected eyesight no worse than 20/60. If your eyesight is not 20/20 uncorrected, it must be correctable to 20/20.

Always keep in mind that your actions have consequences. Avoid getting into any trouble with the law. Due to the sensitive nature of the work, any criminal activity on your record – no matter how small – will automatically disqualify you. Deep background checks are conducted for every applicant. You will not be hired if there is anything in your entire life history that would prevent you from receiving a top-level security clearance.

It is not easy to find a Secret Service agent to talk to about this career. Job shadowing is simply not a possibility. However, the Secret Service does offer an exciting opportunity for a lucky few to experience firsthand what it is like to be a Secret Service agent. Twice a year, the agency conducts its Secret Service Agent-for-a-Week program. Only 15 participants are chosen for each session. The five-day program includes training at the Rowley Training Center and at the Secret Service headquarters location in Washington, DC. The week culminates at the White House when participants are assigned to the Presidential Protective Detail.

The Secret Service offers several other student programs. Positions in these programs are limited, but are worth pursuing since they would provide distinct advantages to those lucky enough to get in. The Secret Service Student Temporary Education Employment Program (STEP) offers federal employment opportunities for degree-seeking students. The agency's Student Career Experience Program offers a two-year work-study program in certain fields of study. In addition, the agency offers unpaid internships through the Student Volunteer Service Program, at which students work a minimum of 12 hours per week.

HISTORY OF THE CAREER

CREATED IN 1865, THE SECRET SERVICE is the oldest federal law enforcement agency in the United States. Although the legislation creating the agency was on Abraham Lincoln's desk the night he was assassinated, its purpose had nothing to do with protection of the president. Instead, it was intended to combat the counterfeit currency problem that occurred during the Civil War. At the time, a whopping one-third of all US currency in circulation was counterfeit.

It was not until 1894 that the US Secret Service took on the role of protectors when it provided part-time guards for President Grover Cleveland on an informal basis. After the assassination of President William McKinley in 1901, Congress officially requested presidential protective services. The following year, the Secret Service assumed the responsibility of providing full-time protection of US presidents. The original White House detail included just two agents. One of those agents, William Craig, became the first agent to die while serving, killed in a road accident while riding in the presidential carriage.

Protective services were expanded in 1917 to include the immediate families of presidents. In that same year, it became a federal crime to make threats against the president. In 1922, President Warren G. Harding requested that a White House police force be formed. Congress placed this force under Secret Service direction in 1930.

An unsuccessful attempt was made on President Harry S. Truman's life in 1950. At the time, Truman was residing across the street at Blair House while the White House was being renovated. Two Puerto Rican nationalists, Oscar Collazo and Griselio Torresola, went to Blair House and when confronted by Truman's protective detail, opened fire. After White House police officer Leslie Coffelt took three shots to the chest and abdomen, he returned fire and killed Torresola with a single shot to his head. Officer Coffelt died from his wounds, making him the only member of the Secret Service to be killed while protecting a president. Shortly after the incident, Congress formalized permanent Secret Service protection for presidents and their immediate families, and expanded services to include the president-elect and the vice president.

In 1962, the vice president-elect was added to a growing list of those under protection. After the assassination of President John F. Kennedy in 1963, increased awareness of the threat to presidents and the people closest to them led Congress to authorize protection for Mrs. Kennedy and her children for two years. This was later extended to lifetime protection of the spouses of deceased presidents unless they remarry, and of the children of former presidents until age 16. Just five years later, the president's brother, Senator Robert F. Kennedy, was assassinated while on the campaign trail. In the wake of this tragedy, Congress once again expanded the circle of protection to include presidential and vice presidential candidates and nominees.

Since the assassination of President Kennedy, only three people under Secret Service protection have been the target of direct assassination attempts: presidential candidate (and Alabama governor) George Wallace in 1972, President Gerald Ford in 1975, and President Ronald Reagan in 1981. All three attempts failed thanks to the work of the Secret Service.

Throughout its history, the Secret Service has been an elite investigative agency. It was started to combat counterfeiting and that is still a primary focus. However, as the nation's financial technologies and systems have evolved, so has the scope of the agency's investigations. In 1984, Congress passed the Comprehensive Crime Control Act, which made numerous types of financial fraud federal violations. The legislation authorized the Secret Service to investigate:

- Credit and debit card fraud
- Computer and telecommunications fraud
- False identification documents
- Electronic funds transfers
- Money laundering
- Electronic funds (EFT) transfers and direct deposit fraud
- Financial institution fraud
- Telemarketing fraud
- ATM fraud

On September 11, 2001, the New York City Field Office of the Secret Service was located at 7 World Trade Center. The office was one of many destroyed in the September 11 attacks. Because of its proximity, Special Agents and other Field Office employees were among the first to respond with help for the victims. Sixty-seven Special Agents helped to set up triage areas and evacuate the towers.

For 138 years, the Secret Service had always been under the umbrella of the US Treasury. That changed on March 1, 2003, when the Secret Service was transferred to the newly created Department of Homeland Security.

On October 26, 2001, President George W. Bush signed into law the USA Patriot Act. The Act directed the Secret Service to establish a nationwide network of task forces to investigate and prevent attacks on financial and critical infrastructures in the US. At the time the Act was passed, there was already one force in New York known as the Electronic Crimes Task Force (ECTF). Using that ECTF as a blueprint, the Secret Service quickly developed a network that brought together federal, state, and local law enforcement, prosecutors, and other relevant leaders that could aid in major investigations. ECTFs now deals with cases that:

- Represent significant economic or community impact
- Involve the participation of multiple-district or transnational organized criminal groups
- Utilize new technology as a means to commit crimes

WHERE YOU WILL WORK

SECRET SERVICE AGENTS ARE AT WORK throughout the nation and overseas. New agents are typically assigned to a field office, which may be anywhere in the United States. There are field offices in every state. Most states have only one, but states with larger populations have more. Texas and California have the most, with nine field offices each. There are also field offices in Guam and Puerto Rico.

Field offices are situated only in the largest cities. Within each field office, there are a number of "resident offices," to service smaller cities and townships.

As agents gain experience, they may be transferred anywhere in the nation or overseas. The Secret Service has field offices in 18 countries. Most have only one office. Only two countries have more than one – Canada has four and France has two.

Special agents on Presidential Protective Detail are posted in Washington, DC, but there is constant travel for these agents. They go wherever the president goes.

Work Schedule

Work in the Secret Service does not fit into the standard 9-to-5, 40-hour work schedule. Special agents, in particular, routinely work long hours. Twelve-hour days are the norm. Secret Service agents in some positions (usually those in protective details), work on rotation, 24 hours on and 24 hours off. Agents often have to travel on extremely short notice. They are expected to be ready to depart within a few hours and be away from home for as long as a month or more.

THE WORK YOU WILL DO

THE SECRET SERVICE IS ONE OF THE nation's most important federal law enforcement organizations. For more than 140 years, it has built highly-skilled teams of individuals who are dedicated to the safety and security of our leaders as well as the country's financial system. Today, the Secret Service is comprised of approximately 3,200 special agents, 1,300 Uniformed Division officers, and more than 2,000 other specialized administrative, professional, and technical support personnel.

Special Agent

Most people associate this job with the Secret Service. It is perceived as glamorous, exciting, and even mysterious. Indeed, Secret Service agents are an elite group that receive one-of-a-kind training to carry out missions. Frequent travel and reassignments to a variety of duty stations are common, occasionally including liaison assignments in foreign countries.

Special agents may be assigned to either the protective or the investigative division. The responsibilities are quite different in each division.

Protection

Secret Service special agents working within the protective division develop and implement strategies to defuse threats to the nation's leaders and other dignitaries. The list of those protected has steadily grown over the past century. It now includes:

- The president and the vice-president and their families
- The president-elect and the vice-president elect
- Former presidents and their wives
- Former presidents' children until their 16th birthday
- Presidential and vice-presidential candidates and their spouses starting four months prior to a general election day
- Visiting heads of states or governments and their spouses
- Distinguished foreign visitors to the United States, such as the Pope or the Dalai Lama
- Representatives of the United States performing special missions outside of the US

Agents may also be assigned to protect special events that require national security, as designated by the Department of Homeland Security.

Special officers perform a wide range of security functions as part of their protective mission. Those assigned to the National Capital Region may be responsible for maintaining designated protective security posts, inspecting safety and emergency equipment of protective vehicles, driving protective vehicles carrying the president or other protected persons, controlling the movement of people into and around protected facilities such as the White House, monitoring communications, and using advanced screening methods to detect and identify high-risk items. In the course of their official duties, special agents are also authorized to make arrests.

When the president or vice president travels – especially when the destination is outside the United States – the mission becomes much more complicated. It is said that every time the president moves, thousands of people are involved. That is not an exaggeration. Preparations start months in advance of the trip, when special agents visit the destination to meet with local agencies. They will need to clear the airspace at the airport for the president's arrival, arrange for a motorcade route through town, identify nearby trauma hospitals (which will never be more than 10 minutes away), and secure safe locations for the president in the event of an attack. Agents run background checks on anyone that might come in contact with the president, either directly or indirectly, such as hotel employees and medical personnel. No one is allowed to offer the president food. When the president travels, he often brings his own food with him, along with a crew of cooks and servers, who buy groceries and prepare food for the president separately in an available kitchen, as Secret Service agents watch to make sure no one interferes.

As the travel date nears, bomb-sniffing dogs are brought in to check each stop on the president's route. Nearby streets are cleared of all parked cars and canopies are set up to protect the president from being exposed while exiting his limousine. Agents perform complete sweeps of all rooms where the president will be, looking for bugging devices and concealed explosives. Nothing is left to chance. They even go as far as taking apart all pictures, looking for anything that might be hidden in the frames. They also place bullet proof plastic over the windows. All electronics are tossed – TVs and phones are removed from and replaced with secure devices. An agent is stationed at each hospital, ready to coordinate with doctors and other agents in the event of a medical emergency.

The day of arrival is intense. Before Air Force One lands, a back-up plane touches down at a secret location. Agents establish multiple security perimeters around the president. Local police form the outer perimeter, Uniform Division officers are stationed in the middle, and Presidential Protective Division agents provide the innermost shield. These last personnel are the men in suits with wires attached to earpieces. They will be on constant alert and remain close to the president for the duration of the visit, ready to confront any threat and die, if need be, in the process.

Newly-appointed agents may be assigned to field offices anywhere in the United States. It is only after gaining several years of field experience that they may be transferred to a protective assignment. It is understood that protection is a young person's game. Special agents rarely stay in protective assignments for more than five years. Following their protective assignment, many agents return to the field or transfer to a headquarters office, a training office, or other Washington, DC-based assignment.

During their careers, special agents may also have the opportunity to work overseas in one of the agency's international field offices. This typically requires foreign language proficiency in order to effectively work alongside the agency's foreign law enforcement counterparts.

Investigation

Only a small percentage of Secret Service agents serve in the protective division. Most are assigned to investigative positions. This is true to the history of the Secret Service, which began as a law enforcement agency to combat the problem of phony money that was being printed and circulated during the Civil War. The Secret Service's investigative mission has grown tremendously since then, due mostly to developments in technology. Today's special agents investigate violations of laws relating to financial crimes such as credit card and access device fraud, as well as computer-based attacks on the nation's banking and telecommunications.

The Secret Service originally set out to investigate and mitigate the counterfeiting of paper money only. Coins were added a few years later. Now the agency handles the counterfeiting of US Treasury checks, US postage stamps, Department of Agriculture food stamps, and foreign currency that is counterfeited on American soil.

Secret Service criminal investigations now cover anything connected to financial systems, financial institutions, and technology-related activities. This includes a wide range of offenses, but the most common are:

- Computer and telecommunications fraud
- Check fraud
- Bank fraud
- Credit card and debit card fraud
- Passport/Visa fraud
- False identification
- Identity Theft
- Money Laundering
- Computer and telecommunications fraud
- Automated payment system and ATM fraud

The Uniformed Division

The Uniformed Division's mission is protective. Unlike special agents who provide personal protection, uniformed officers protect facilities and venues that need to be secured. Agents serving in the Uniformed Division originally provided physical protection for the White House complex and the vice president's residence at the Naval Observatory. The Division has grown over the years both in size and in scope of responsibility. It now provides security for a number of other key sites in Washington, DC, such as the main Treasury Building and Annex as well as many embassies in the Washington area.

Uniformed Division officers also work outside of the nation's capital. They may travel throughout the country or abroad in support of presidential, vice presidential and foreign head of state government missions. Again, their role is to protect venues and locations, not the dignitaries themselves. For example, if the president wanted to speak to workers in an auto plant, Uniformed Division officers and their support teams would secure the factory and control access to the facility.

Uniformed Division officers typically come from military and law enforcement backgrounds. Their initial assignments may be routine in nature, but as their careers progress, they may be selected to participate in one of several specialized units, including:

Canine Unit uses highly trained dogs to perform security sweeps and respond to bomb threats and suspicious packages.

Emergency Response Team responds to threats to the White House and other protected facilities with coordinated tactical measures.

Counter Sniper Team uses keen observation, sighting equipment, and high-performance weapons to provide a secure environment for anyone under protection.

Motorcade Support Unit takes part in motorcades by providing motorcycle tactical support for official vehicles.

Crime Scene Search Unit photographs, collects, and processes physical and latent evidence.

Office of Training includes classroom instructors, firearms training experts, and recruiters.

Special Operations Section is assigned to protect the White House complex. This includes routine as well as special duties and functions, such as state dinners, Rose Garden ceremonies, and public tours of the White House.

Administrative, Professional, and Technical (APT)

The work of the Secret Service is multifaceted and therefore requires a diverse range of skills and talent. People are recruited from all segments of the American population to fill positions in the agency's administrative, professional and technical (APT) division.

Administrative positions cover a wide range of duties associated with management, administration, clerical, and administrative support. Examples of jobs in this area include analytical research, writing, and training development.

Professional positions usually involve work within a field of science. There are also many professional specialists who are experts in a specialized field. This could include, for example, forensic psychiatry, chemistry, or linguistics.

Technical positions are found within all areas of the Secret Service. People in these jobs provide direct support for the law enforcement agents as well as professional or administrative personnel. Assignments outside of general IT tend to be non-routine, requiring broad practical knowledge. Fingerprint specialists and access control coordinators fall into this category.

There are dozens of different APT jobs, each of which is critical to the overall success of the agency's missions. Here are a few examples of APT job titles:

- Forensic Photographer
- Writer/Editor
- Civil Engineer
- Research Psychologist
- Social Worker
- Access Control Coordinator
- Information Technology Specialist

- Document Analyst
- Materials Engineer
- Public Affairs Specialist
- Financial Management Specialist
- Criminal Research Specialists

In addition to the many salaried employees, the Secret Service employs consultants, experts, and various independent contractors on a temporary, per-project basis.

STORIES OF THE SECRET SERVICE

I Am a Special Agent

"I am assigned to protective services in the National Capital Region, which generally means I help protect the president and vice president of the United States. It is an enjoyable job that I am honored to do.

There is no such thing as a typical day in the Secret Service. My responsibilities range dramatically from personal protection to managing and training new agents to advance work related to protection. I especially enjoy doing advance, bringing White House personnel together to maintain operational readiness and solving problems. I also spend a good deal of time in assorted formal and informal classes. Even though my career thus far has spanned nearly 10 years, I still continue to learn about security protocols and counter surveillance. I enjoy learning new techniques that could help me do a better job. The training, both initial and ongoing, is unmatched.

This can be very challenging work. I am frequently tasked with difficult assignments that require all my skills and energy to successfully complete the mission. The most challenging part of the job is the time it takes away from family. I typically work 12 hours a day, every day. Then there are the trips that take me away from home for extended periods of time. When I get a call for emergency travel, I have to get packed and out to the airport within six hours, and I usually have no idea how long I'll be gone. It takes absolute dedication without question, but it also requires infinite patience and understanding from my family.

The Secret Service is a terrific organization. I get to work with highly-skilled, exceptional people. It is a fast-paced environment in an unpredictable world. Each day can bring plenty of unexpected events that have to be handled in a calm and orderly manner. It's not always easy, but I get plenty in return – mostly prestige and pride in what I do."

I Am a Student Intern

"My internship is in counterfeit, but I am not involved in taking in counterfeit money or investigating its source. Instead, my duties are mostly clerical. Typical tasks include filing, answering the phone, and inputting data into computer databases. This might sound dull, but this has been a great experience. I have learned that every person here has something to contribute, and only when we work as a team does the job get done.

Collaboration is an important aspect of any work within the Secret Service. I have learned a great deal about the importance of teamwork by watching the Special Agents. They help each other constantly by reviewing cases, going over case facts, backing each other up on surveillance, and teaching each other new techniques.

I would strongly recommend looking into being an intern if you are considering a career in the Secret Service. Having the opportunity to be a part of the most elite law enforcement organization in the world is invaluable. The internship program is designed for students who want to explore career options and get a better understanding of the nature of the organization. It is a volunteer position, meaning there is no pay, but it does offer academic credit. Interns are expected to work a minimum of 12 hours per week for at least one semester or summer session. That is plenty of time to develop some professional skills and make connections that will be useful no matter what you end up doing career wise. To get involved, visit the nearest field office."

PERSONAL QUALITIES

THE SECRET SERVICE HAS VERY HIGH STANDARDS. THE AGENCY ONLY HIRES PEOPLE OF THE highest caliber, all of whom are expected to demonstrate the Secret Service's five core values: justice, duty, courage, honesty, and loyalty. Most important is a passion for public service and a genuine concern for the safety of the country's leaders and their families. In addition, agents must be able to handle extreme stress while maintaining a professional attitude. To be successful in this career, you will need a number of other personal qualifications, including the following:

Dedication

Secret Service agents often work under excessive pressure. The work is sometimes extremely dangerous with no time for second guessing or thinking of one's own safety. Agents in protective assignments must be so dedicated to the well-being of the person protected, that they are ready to risk their own lives in support of the mission. Dedication also means being ready and willing to move anywhere in the US or in the world. Orders to travel often come down on extremely short notice. This can mean being away from family for weeks or even months. Even at home, the work can require long and staggered hours, putting a strain on one's personal life. In the Secret Service, it is understood that the mission comes first, last, and always.

A Sharp Intellect

All agents have above-average intelligence. Having a poor score on an intelligence test is enough to disqualify you from being accepted into the agency. Secret Service agents must possess excellent observational skills, memory, and judgement, regardless of their positions. They are responsible for recognizing potential dangers that most people would miss and remembering all the tiny details involved in the crimes they are investigating. Protective agents, in particular, need to be intelligent, aware, and mentally and emotionally stable. During a series of oral tests and interviews, recruiters look for those who are well spoken and have an excellent command of the English language.

Physical Fitness

All agents need to be in excellent shape. The rigors of working in protective details are particularly demanding. If your goal is to become a Secret Service agent, you need to work hard to get in top physical condition long before applying to the agency. Prospective new hires are put through a series of physical fitness tests that evaluate both strength and stamina.

Team Work

Being a good team member is essential for this career. In the Secret Service, nobody can do the job alone. You must have respect for your colleagues and possess the interpersonal skills required to work well with others. At the same time, you should be able to think independently. You should have the confidence to make snap decisions when necessary, which may be of a life-or-death nature.

Do you have some specialized skills **Special Skills**

? That could be your path of entry. The Secret Service has a wide range of positions to fill and is always on the lookout for people who are the best in their respective fields. For example, the ability to solve codes is always useful. But perhaps the most sought after skill is fluency in a foreign language. Being able to speak one foreign language is a distinct hiring advantage. Someone who has mastered several languages is of immediate interest to the agency.

ATTRACTIVE FEATURES

THIS IS A JOB THAT CAN BE DIFFICULT and even dangerous at times, but working for one of the preeminent law enforcement agencies in the world can be as rewarding as it is challenging. Secret Service employees are unanimous in their assertion that it is an honor and a privilege to be a part of that organization. In addition to the overall job satisfaction and prestige, there are a number of other benefits to working in the Secret Service.

You get to work with outstanding people. The Secret Service only hires the best of the best, from entry-level positions to executive leadership roles. Every one of them has led an exemplary life and is carefully selected for their skills and talents. One of the most enjoyable parts of the job is getting to know the agents and other colleagues. You will find they are very professional, positive, conscientious, motivated, and proud of their contributions.

The pay is generous and the benefits are enviable. Special agents earn salaries in the six-figure range after a few years of experience. There is also a variety of bonuses offered to agents that can boost overall compensation considerably. Uniformed officers and other personnel are also paid well, though their paychecks are not as high as those of agents. All Secret Service personnel are federal government employees, which means they get great benefits.

Life in the Secret Service is certainly not boring. There is no such thing as a typical day. It is a fast-paced environment that can bring plenty of unexpected events. Each day brings a new set of challenges that keeps the work from ever becoming routine. Positions are very diverse and responsibilities range dramatically among them. There are opportunities to take advantage of the agency's many training programs to move into new areas.

There are opportunities to travel. Depending on the career phase, extensive travel may be required. Most Secret Service agents travel frequently throughout the nation in the early years of their careers. Reassignments to a variety of duty stations are also common. There will likely be travel outside the United States. Special agents with foreign language proficiency travel the world extensively to liaison with foreign dignitaries or accompany the president or vice president during visits to other countries. Any Secret Service employee with multiple language skills may be stationed in a foreign office.

The Secret Service offers an excellent opportunity to serve your country and perform meaningful work. You will be able to witness history being made every day. It is a life changing experience.

UNATTRACTIVE ASPECTS

THERE IS A COMMON MISCONCEPTION that working for the Secret Service is glamorous. The reality is that it is a very difficult job that is often stressful and sometimes dangerous. For every hour that an agent spends with the president, flying on Air Force One, there are 100 hours spent standing somewhere being uncomfortable. The Secret Service is known for providing unsurpassed training, but that training goes on forever for those on protective details.

The hardest part of being an agent is the hours. The hours are typically long – that is why there is a bonus to compensate for overtime. Some of the time is being on duty, some of it is spent on the target range, or in training classes. You will have few days off. Emergency travel makes regular sleep almost impossible. Agents experience jet lag and malnourishment from repeatedly crossing multiple time zones.

The work/life balance is not good. It is expected that the job comes first and you must plan your life around your work. That means you will need to make personal sacrifices. The constant time away from home can be a real problem for those with families.

It is hard to get into the Secret Service. This is no ordinary job. It takes a long time to get through the application process. Even after working hard and making it through college with excellent grades, a single misstep will put you out of the running.

EDUCATION AND TRAINING

IT IS POSSIBLE TO JOIN THE SECRET SERVICE without a college education. Uniformed division officer positions do not require a formal education beyond a high school diploma or equivalent. Candidates must also pass the Police Officer Selection Test. The selection standards are high for both uniformed agents and special agents, however, the bar is even higher for special agents. Eligibility for a special agent position starts with a bachelor's degree from an accredited college or university. Candidates must have a superior academic record, evidenced by a high GPA, graduate in the top third of their class, or be a member of a national academic honors society. Applicants for both positions must also pass an extensive series of tests, both mental and physical, and pass background checks.

Aspiring Secret Service special agents can apply for jobs at two different levels: GL-7 and GL-9. The requirements, responsibilities, and pay are lower at the GL-7 level. To qualify at the GL-7 level, candidates must have maintained at least a 3.5 GPA in all college courses related to the major and a 3.0 in all other classes within the degree program. Those who fail to meet these exceptional academic requirements are still eligible to apply if they successfully complete at least 18 months of graduate studies. Technically, any major is acceptable, but the best choices are those that provide students with knowledge and skills that are closely related to work in law enforcement. Good majors to consider include criminology, criminal justice, homeland security, or protection management. These degree programs typically include courses in law enforcement, criminal justice administration, crime scene investigation, and intelligence.

Many Secret Service positions are at the GL-9 level. To be eligible for these jobs, candidates must have a master's degree, a law degree (LLB or JD), or at least four years of specialized experience carrying out investigations, conducting surveillance or undercover activities, or organizing evidence for prosecutors.

Secret Service Training

The Secret Service provides two training programs for new recruits – the 10-week Basic Criminal Investigator Training program and a 17-week special agent basic training course. In order to get an assignment, prospective agents must pass both programs in the first attempt. There are no second chances. Those who fail will not be hired.

The initial 10-week program takes place at the Federal Law Enforcement Training Center (FLETC) in Glynco, Georgia. The program is designed to provide new agents with a foundation in investigation techniques and criminal law. Topics covered include investigative techniques, firearms, first aid, laws of arrest, police procedures, and criminal law.

The 17-week special agent-training course is conducted at the James J. Rowley Training Center near Washington, DC. It is here that agent trainees gain a deeper knowledge of the organization, including its policies and procedures. In the classroom, trainees receive basic and advanced instruction in physical protection, emergency medicine, combating counterfeiting, financial device fraud, and financial criminal activity. Training outside the classroom is focused on physical skills and includes extensive training in physical fitness, marksmanship, and water survival skills.

Continuous Advanced Training

Training never stops for Secret Service agents. Periodic training for all agents includes emergency medicine refresher courses, firearms requalification, and advanced criminal investigations training. Those who have protective assignments are also required to participate in specialized crisis training simulations. These are regularly scheduled and ongoing. Though not required, all agents are encouraged to attend training sponsored by other law enforcement agencies. All employees of the Secret Service, including those who are not agents, must periodically complete courses in personal development, ethics, and diversity.

EARNINGS

SECRET SERVICE SPECIAL AGENTS ARE PAID WELL with annual salaries ranging from about $105,000 to $140,000. According to salary reports provided by employees, an agent is typically paid around $120,000. Most agents receive annual raises after positive annual reviews, along with the additional benefits that come with promotions.

Secret Service agents are hired at one of two pay grades, GL-7 or GL-9, depending on education, academic achievement, and experience. These are considered entry level. An experienced agent can reach GL-13. Starting salaries for special agents (GL-7 or GL-9) will range from $54,000 to $94,000 annually depending on the initial duty station.

Agents working on specific federal investigations have the potential to receive added bonuses for their work. Special agents also receive an additional 25 percent Law Enforcement Availability Pay (LEAP) to compensate for the extra hours and nontraditional schedules they work. Locality pay is another source of additional pay. The amount of the locality pay varies. For example, the salary of a special agent working in Atlanta includes a locality pay of about 20 percent, while those working in Chicago receive a locality pay of over 25 percent.

Special agents with foreign language skills are eligible for a one time recruitment bonus of 25 percent of basic annual pay, but only after testing for foreign language proficiency. The Secret Service also has a Foreign Language Cash Award Program, which pays a cash award of up to 5 percent of basic pay to employees who make substantial use of one or more foreign languages in the performance of official duties.

Officers in the Uniformed Division receive starting salaries of around $50,000, according to the most recent information from the Secret Service. Unlike special agents, Uniformed Division officers are paid hourly and therefore do not qualify for locality pay or LEAP. They do, however, get overtime compensation at the rate of time and one-half, or through compensatory time off. Their uniforms and equipment are furnished at no cost.

Bonuses and Benefits

As federal government workers, Secret Service employees receive excellent bonuses and benefits packages. Special agents, Uniformed Division officers, and those in APT positions are eligible for a number of benefits, which include:

- Health benefits
- Group life insurance
- Long-term care insurance
- Thrift savings plan
- Comprehensive retirement benefits
- Benevolent fund
- Paid federal holidays
- Annual leave (at the rate of 13 to 26 days per year)
- Sick leave (at the rate of 13 days per year without limit)
- Federal flexible spending account

OPPORTUNITIES

CURRENTLY, THE SECRET SERVICE HAS ABOUT 6,500 EMPLOYEES. This includes 3,200 special agents and 1,300 uniformed division officers. An additional 2,000 personnel work in technical, administrative, and other support functions. While there is no specific data to indicate how many jobs might open up for new Secret Service agents or officers, the outlook is generally good. The Secret Service is not expected to add many new positions, but opportunities will continue to exist for qualified candidates.

Historically, most jobs have become available through attrition and retirements. In the coming years, however, there are two reasons why career opportunities may be on the rise. First, is the growing number of political figures that need protection. It is not only the president and vice president and their families who are protected by the Secret Service. Those protected now also include presidential and vice presidential candidates and nominees, and foreign heads of state while visiting the US. Plus, all former presidents and vice presidents along with their spouses are provided protection for life.

The other reason for job growth involves cyber-crime. More agents knowledgeable about technology are needed to create new policies and develop ways to track cyber criminals and prevent computer hackers from getting into federal government files.

Competition for jobs in the Secret Service is tough, but once in the door, there is plenty of room for advancement. Secret service agents typically start their careers with an assignment in a field office. The field assignment usually lasts six to eight years, after which the agent is given a protective assignment. Agents may be assigned to guard one specific political figure and their family or be assigned to the temporary assignment staff, which will have them protecting various people as needed. After three to five years in protection, agents may advance to investigative positions. The Secret Service is known for moving agents around frequently in an effort to find the position that best suits individual skills and strengths.

Most positions are offered through field offices and are located in the United States. However, opportunities do exist outside the U.S. Secret Service agents who are fluent in other languages can be assigned to overseas posts.

GETTING STARTED

GETTING A JOB WITH THE US SECRET SERVICE is not easy. The selection process is extremely competitive and there is no shortcut to the front of the line. Networking will not help. It does not matter who you know. You will not find help wanted ads for agents in the newspaper and unless you are a police officer or in the military, no recruiter will be calling. So how do you get hired by the Secret Service? It all starts with an application, which you can get from the nearest Secret Service field office. You can also apply online through USAJobs.gov. This website allows applicants to submit résumés and supporting documentation, and to check on the status of their applications.

Before filling out an application, make sure you meet the basic qualifications. If you do not meet these qualifications, no one will even look at your application. These qualifications include:

- A college degree or a combination of college and law enforcement work experience, with a background in criminal investigation
- A record of superior academic achievement or prior relevant experience
- Be between the ages of 21 and 37
- US citizenship
- A current, valid driver license
- At least 20/60 vision, correctable to 20/20
- Registered with the Selective Service System or have proof of exemption

Remember, these are just the basics to get your application looked at. If you meet the basic eligibility requirements, you will be put through a series of very specific steps including a series of competency tests to determine if you have what it takes to get the job done. The first test is the Treasury Enforcement Agent Examination. This is a basic abilities test that evaluates reading comprehension, reasoning, math skills, and investigative abilities. Your writing skills will also be tested in a report writing assessment. The entire exam is a written test. If you pass, you will be put through a number of oral interviews designed to assess your verbal communications skills and your ability and determination to succeed in the Secret Service.

The next step will test your physical fitness. Any career in law enforcement can be physically demanding, but the rigors associated with dignitary protection require a high level of physical fitness.

The Secret Service physical fitness test consists of push-ups, sit-ups, chin-ups, and a 1.5-mile run. Test scores are based on the number of push-ups, sit-ups, and chin-ups and how fast the run is completed. If you appear to be physically fit, you will be put through medical testing to make sure you are in good health. Doctors will give you a physical examination, checking vision, hearing, blood pressure, heart function, and more. Drug testing is also done. If everything checks out, you will be one step closer to your dream job.

Next comes a full background investigation. All Secret Service agents must be able to obtain a top-secret clearance. This is a lengthy process that can take up to nine months. Deep background checks will probe your employment history, police records, credit and financial history, and military records. Past employers and superior officers will be interviewed. Agents are expected to be of impeccable character. Any evidence to the contrary, such as past-due debts, student loan defaults, prior felony arrests, or past drug use, will disqualify you from ever joining the Secret Service. Applicants must also pass a polygraph exam. If the polygraph examiner detects any deception, you are automatically disqualified.

Going through this lengthy hiring process can take a year or more. If you make it through, congratulations are in order. But you are not done yet. Accepted recruits are sent to the Secret Service training centers where they undergo a total of 27 weeks of extensive training. If they successfully complete training on the first attempt, they will be officially hired and given their first assignments.

ASSOCIATION

- **Association of Former Agents: US Secret Service**
  https://www.oldstar.org

WEBSITES

- **Student Volunteer Service Program**
  www.secretservice.gov/join/diversity/students

- **Secret Service Agent-for-a-Week**
  https://whitehouse.gov1.info/secretservice

- **United States Secret Service**
  http://www.secretservice.gov

- **US Secret Service Employment Opportunities**
  https://www.usajobs.gov

Copyright 2017 Institute For Career Research
Careers Internet Database Website www.careers-internet.org
Careers Reports on Amazon
www.amazon.com/Institute-For-Career-Research/e/B007DO4Y9E
For information please email service@careers-internet.org

www.ingramcontent.com/pod-product-compliance
Lightning Source LLC
Chambersburg PA
CBHW061240180526
45170CB00003B/1375